Do you like to play games? Just about everybody does.

Let's try one. Let's play a game called make-believe.

Are you ready?

Here we go.

Close your eyes real tight. Do you see any light at all? If you do, then your eyes are not closed enough. Close them tighter, and put your hands over them too.

Now think about the nicest and the most beautiful place you have ever seen. Make believe you can see it again.

Did that place have flowers?

Was there an ocean or a lake or maybe there was just a little stream of water?

something good to eat?
How about your mommy
and daddy?
Were
they there
too?

Was there sunshine?

Were birds singing? Did you see them?

Now open your eyes again, and take your hands away.

Wasn't that fun? But the best part of playing the game called make-believe is that you see things with your eyes closed.

That was a good game to

play. So let's play it all over again. Only this time we will do it another way.

Are you ready?

Close your eyes.

Close them tighter than that.

Cover your eyes like before. Don't let one speck of light in.

Now
think about that
same place again. It's
the nicest and prettiest place
you ever saw. It is a place
where you had fun.

Now try to make it nicer.
Make it the most beautiful
place you have ever seen,
even better than before.

Are the trees bigger?

What color are the leaves?

Do you see any animals? Are there lions and tigers? And are they real tame so you can pet them? They should be.

What about houses? Do you see any?

Remember to keep your eyes closed.

What do the houses look like? Make them the most beautiful houses you can think of. Are they castles?

Now it is time to rest again. Open your eyes, and take your hands away.

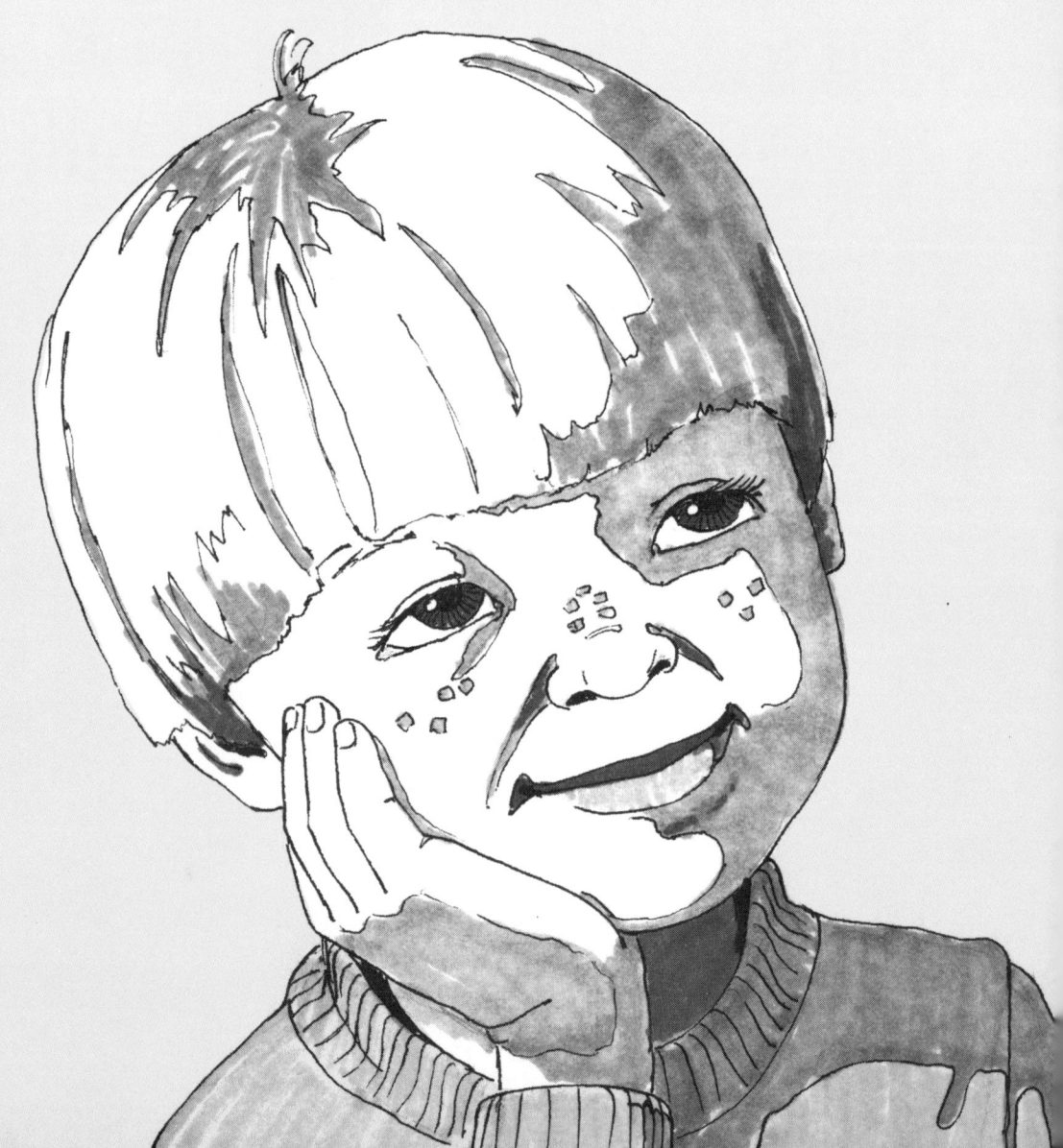

Wasn't that game a lot of fun?

Oh, did you see a city when you had your eyes closed? There was one. What kind of a city was it?

Did you look at its streets?

Close your eyes again.

Tighter! Don't use your hands this time.

Now, make-believe you see that city.

Look closer.

Keep your eyes closed.

Well, now, would you look at that! The streets are made of real gold. Do you see them?

And look at all the bright colors under the city, way down below the golden streets. Why, there are all the colors you can think of. Do you see them?

Name the colors that you see. Do it out loud.

LOOK! There is a river. And what a beautiful river it is too. Think about how good it must taste. Did you ever drink water from a river? Most rivers are dirty, but this one is clean.

Look again! There are trees down by the river. And people are picking fruit from one special tree. What kind of fruit are they picking? Now they are eating it. Look at that fruit real close.

Keep your eyes closed. That fruit looks like gold and silver. Isn't it beautiful?

Wouldn't you like to eat some too?

Open your eyes again. Wasn't that fun?

But here is a secret that isn't a secret at all. There really are houses more beautiful than anything you ever saw. And there are streets made of real gold.

Now, where do you think that place is?

Why, it's where God lives, and He named the place heaven. Have you heard about it?

And do you know what? You can live there with Him forever if you want to. So can Mommy and Daddy. Just think, beyond the moon, way past the sun, and stars, is a special home that belongs to you if—

And that little word "if" is so important, because "if" you love Jesus with all your heart, above everything and